ACTIVITY CARDS
FOR

HELPING CHILDREN
LEARN MATHEMATICS
Fifth Edition

Robert E. Reys
University of Missouri

Marilyn N. Suydam
Ohio State University

Mary M. Lindquist
Columbus State University

Nancy L. Smith
Emporia State University

Allyn and Bacon

Boston • London • Toronto • Sydney • Tokyo • Singapore

ISBN 0-205-27194-4

Printed in the United States of America

10 9 8 7 6 5 4 3 2   02 01 00 99 98

Table of Contents

Helping Children Learn Mathematics

This set of Activity Cards is provided for use with children as you help them learn mathematics. Each Activity Card has been used with children in one form or another, but you may wish to modify it to suit the needs of the students you are teaching. Your are granted permission to make limited copies of any or all of these Activity Cards for use with your students.

The Activity Cards are neither a complete nor a continuous sequence of instructional activities. Rather, the activities provide a range of different ways to promote the learning of mathematics. No specific grade levels or mathematical topic labels are included on the Activity Cards, so you are free to decide when, where and how to use them. We invite you to "pick and choose" activities that you think would be appropriate, interesting and useful in promoting mathematical thinking. For example, these Activity Cards may be used as a master for an overhead transparency to guide a whole class lesson, discussed in small groups, or explored independently by children.

Earlier editions of *Helping Children Learn Mathematics* have contained a variety of activity cards. Over the years, we have received many thoughtful suggestions from pre-service and inservice teachers about ways to improve or strengthen our book. One frequent theme has been to increase the size of the Activity Cards so they can be more easily used with children. This book of activity cards includes cards that we think you will find particularly useful with children.

We invite you to continue to share suggestions related to *Helping Children Learn Mathematics,* and the Activity Cards in particular. Please let us know what you like. Also, please let us know what you don't like, as well as your ideas for improving these instructional resources.

Robert E. Reys
Marilyn N. Suydam
Mary M. Lindquist
Nancy L. Smith

Name: _____

Class: _____

Patterns with Blocks

▼ Each of these boxes holds 16 blocks:

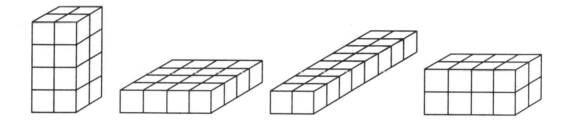

▼ Take 24 blocks. Make as many different boxes as you can.

- How many different boxes did you make?

- Tell how many layers each box had.

- Tell how many blocks are in each layer.

▼ Suppose that you have 4 piles of blocks and that all the blocks in the pile must be used:

Pile A has 16 blocks.   Pile B has 25 blocks.

Pile C has 36 blocks.   Pile D has 50 blocks.

- Which pile of blocks would you choose to build the most different boxes? Tell why.

- Which pile would you choose to build the fewest different boxes? Tell why.

Name: _____

Class: _____

Using Patterns

▼ These drawings suggest some patterns:

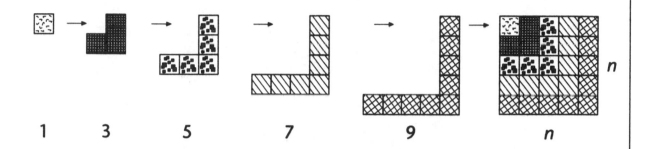

1   3   5   7   9   n

- Look the drawings over carefully and describe a pattern.

- If you were building the "next square," describe the next backward "L" you would need.

- Use a pattern to predict the sum when $n = 10$. Check to see if your prediction is correct.

▼ Now use a pattern to predict the sum when $n = 20$.

▼ Tell how you would express this relationship as a formula.

Name: _____

Class: _____

Who Am I?

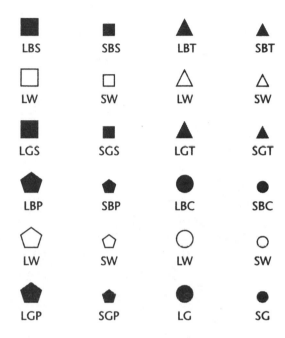

■	■	▲	▲
LBS	SBS	LBT	SBT
□	□	△	△
LW	SW	LW	SW
■	■	▲	▲
LGS	SGS	LGT	SGT
⬟	⬟	●	●
LBP	SBP	LBC	SBC
⬠	⬠	○	○
LW	SW	LW	SW
⬟	⬟	●	●
LGP	SGP	LG	SG

▼ Match me with the attribute blocks shown here:

A. I have three sides.
I am blue.
I am large.

Who am I? _____

B. I am black or white.
I have three sides.
I am not large.

Who am I? _____

C. I am not blue.
I am not white.
I have five sides.
I am small.

Who am I? _____

D. I am not large.
I have more than
four sides.
I am gray.

Who am I? _____

• Which of these describe more than one piece? _____

• Which of these describe the same piece? _____

▼ Your turn:

Pick a piece to describe and play "Who Am I?"
with another person.

Helping Children Learn Mathematics, Fifth Edition, © 1998 by Allyn and Bacon

Name: _____

Class: _____

Alike-and-Difference Trains

Each car in a train is like the car it follows in two ways, *or* it is different from the car it follows in two ways.

▼ Find the alike-and-difference pattern in each train, and describe the missing car:

Train A ▲ ▲ ▲ ▲ △ ____

Train B ▲ ⬟ ⬟ ● ○ ____

Train C ● ○ ____ ▲ ● ⬠

Train D ● △ ⬠ ● ○ ____

• Which of these are one-difference trains? _____

• Which of these are two-difference trains? _____

▼ Your turn:

• Begin with ■. Make a train (with at least six cars) in which each car has exactly one attribute different from the car it follows. Compare your train with someone's train. Are they the same?

• Begin with ■. Make a train (with at least six cars) in which each car has exactly one attribute like the car it follows. Compare your train with another train. Tell how they are alike.

Name: _____

Class: _____

Hunting for Numbers

▼ Look at this chart:

1	2	3	4	5	6	7	8	9	10
11	12	13	14	15	16	17	18	19	20
21	22	23	24	25	26	27	28	29	30
31	32	33	34	35	36	37	38	39	40
41	42	■	44	45	46	47	48	49	50
51	52	53	54	55	56	57	58	59	60
61	62	63	64	65	66	67	68	69	70
71	72	73	74	75	76	77	78	79	80
81	82	83	84	85	86	87	88	89	90
91	92	93	94	95	96	97	98	99	100

- What is hidden by the ■ ?
- What number is after ■ ?
- What number is before the ■ ?

▼ Put a ● on any number.

- Begin at ● : Count forward five.
- Begin at ● again: Count backward five.

▼ Put a ▲ on a different number.

- Begin at ▲ : Count forward five.
- Begin at ▲ again: Count backward five.

▼ Tell about any patterns you see.

Helping Children Learn Mathematics, Fifth Edition, © 1998 by Allyn and Bacon

Name: _____

Class: _____

Decide If It's Up or Down

- Circle the if the number of dots is *more than* the number symbol.

- Circle the if the number of dots is *less than* the number symbol.

5

10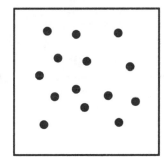

5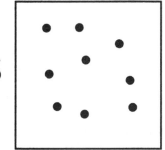

10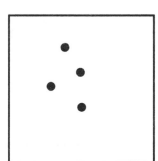

Decide If It's  Up or Down

- Circle the 👍 if the number of dots is *more than* the number symbol.

- Circle the 👎 if the number of dots is *less than* the number symbol.

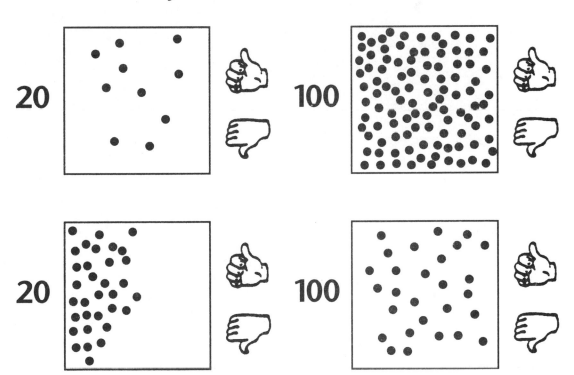

Name: _____

Class: _____

Find That Number!

▼ Use this hundred chart:

1	2	3	4	5	6	7	8	9	10
11	12	13	14	15	16	17	18	19	20
21	22	23	24	25	26	27	28	29	30
31	32	33	34	35	36	37	38	39	40
41	42	43	44	45	46	47	48	49	50
51	52	53	54	55	56	57	58	59	60
61	62	63	64	65	66	67	68	69	70
71	72	73	74	75	76	77	78	79	80
81	82	83	84	85	86	87	88	89	90
91	92	93	94	95	96	97	98	99	100

- Pick a number and count 10 more. Where did you stop? _____

- Pick a number and count 20 more. Where did you stop? _____

- Pick a number and count 50 more. Predict where you would stop. _____

- Tell how you can use the hundred chart to mentally add 30 to a number.

▼ Here is only a part of a hundred chart:

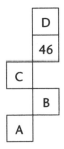

- Use what you know about a hundred chart to find the values:

- A_____   B_____   C_____   D_____

- Tell how you found C.

- Could you find C in more than one way? Explain your answer.

Name: _____

Class: _____

What's in a Score?

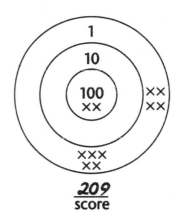

My darts landed on the x's. Check out my score.

1
10
100 ×× ××
×× ××
×××
××

209
score

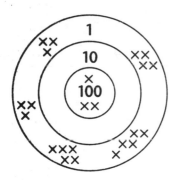

_____
score

_____
score

What is the score here?

1
10
100

204
score

1
10
100

402
score

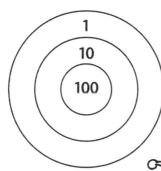

Show how these scores might have been made. Then show them another way!

Name: _____

Class: _____

Hitting Hundreds

▼ Which target will you hit?

Write what your 🖩 shows.

Start	Rule	Which target?		Guess	Check
20	+100	(200)	(220)	_____	_____
35	+100	(335)	(500)	_____	_____
41	+100	(410)	(441)	_____	_____
86	+100	(586)	(580)	_____	_____
97	+100	(897)	(970)	_____	_____
169	+100	(469)	(696)	_____	_____
123	+100	(321)	(323)	_____	_____

Name: _____

Class: _____

The Power of 10 on the Hundred Chart

1	2	3	4	5	6	7	8	9	10
11	12	13	14	15	16	17	18	19	20
21	22	23	24	25	26	27	28	29	30
31	32	33	34	35	36	37	38	39	40
41	42	43	44	45	46	47	48	49	50
51	52	53	54	55	56	57	58	59	60
61	62	63	64	65	66	67	68	69	70
71	72	73	74	75	76	77	78	79	80
81	82	83	84	85	86	87	88	89	90
91	92	93	94	95	96	97	98	99	100

▼ Count by 10:

- Start on any square in the first three rows.

- Count forward 10 squares, and tell where you stopped.

- Start at a different square, and count forward 10 squares.

- After you have done this several times, tell about a pattern that you found.

- Describe a quick way to count "ten more" on this hundred chart.

▼ Count by 9:

- Start on any square in the first three rows.

- Count forward 9 squares. Tell where you stopped.

- After you have done this several times, tell about a pattern that you found.

- Describe a quick way to count "nine more" on this chart.

▼ Connect the patterns:

- Does knowing how to count by 10 help you count by 9?

Helping Children Learn Mathematics, Fifth Edition, © 1998 by Allyn and Bacon

Name: _____

Class: _____

The Power of 10
on the Thousand Chart

10	20	30	40	50	60	70	80	90	100
110	120	130	140	150	160	170	180	190	200
210	220	230	240	250	260	270	280	290	300
310	320	330	340	350	360	370	380	390	400
410	420	430	440	450	460	470	480	490	500
510	520	530	540	550	560	570	580	590	600
610	620	630	640	650	660	670	680	690	700
710	720	730	740	750	760	770	780	790	800
810	820	830	840	850	860	870	880	890	900
910	920	930	940	950	960	970	980	990	1000

▼ Count by 10:

- Start on any square in the first three rows.

- Count forward 10 squares and tell where you stopped.

- Start at a different square, and count forward 10 squares.

- After you have done this several times, tell about a pattern that you fo

- Describe a quick way to count "a hundred more" on this thousand ch

▼ Count by 100:

- Tell how you could use the thousand chart to add 300 to 240.

- Tell how you could use the thousand chart to add 290 to 240.

▼ Connect the charts:

- Tell how using the hundred chart helps you use the thousand chart?

Helping Children Learn Mathematics, Fifth Edition, © 1998 by Allyn and Bacon

How Big is BIG?

A million . . .

- dollars is _____ $1,000 bills.

- days is about _____ years.

- hours is about _____ years.

- dollar bills would weigh about _____ .

- miles is about _____ .

A billion . . .

- dollars is _____$1,000 bills.

- seconds is about _____ .

- people is _____ .

Helping Children Learn Mathematics, Fifth Edition, © 1998 by Allyn and Bacon

Name: _____

Class: _____

Deciding Which Way to Round

▼ These prices could be rounded different ways:

- How many ways can these prices be rounded?

- How would you "round" these prices if you wanted to round them to the same number?

- What would you "round to" in deciding how much money is needed to make each purchase?

▼ Try this:

Carl Furillo (Brooklyn Dodgers) had a lifetime batting average of .2994 in the major leagues, yet he is not considered a .300 hitter.

- How do you think he would like averages to be "rounded"?

▼ Your turn:

Describe a situation when you would want to round up; to round down.

Name: _____

Class: _____

Picking Up Sticks

How many different ways can you find to hold up 7 dots with dot sticks? Show them here.

7 dots

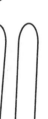

or   or

or

What dot sticks will go here to make 12 dots?

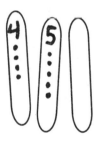

12 dots

▼ Decide what sticks are missing. Fill them in.

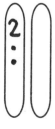   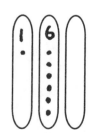   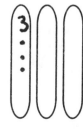   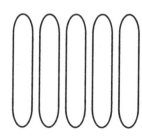

8 dots   9 dots   6 dots   15 dots

Helping Children Learn Mathematics, Fifth Edition, © 1998 by Allyn and Bacon

Rectangles and More Rectangles!

▼ How many ways can you make a rectangle with this many cubes?

▼ List the ways:

1 cube ☐

_____   _____

2 cubes ☐ ☐

_____   _____

_____

3 cubes ☐ ☐ ☐

_____   _____

_____

4 cubes ☐ ☐ ☐ ☐

_____   _____

_____

_____

5 cubes ☐ ☐ ☐ ☐ ☐

_____   _____

_____

8 cubes ☐ ☐ ☐ ☐ ☐ ☐ ☐ ☐

_____

_____

_____

_____

Name: _____

Class: _____

How Many Squares in a Rectangle?

▼ Draw a 3 × 4 rectangle:

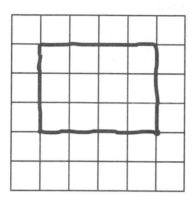

That's 3 × 4 or 4 × 3. It's a rectangle with 12 squares.

▼ Your turn:

Draw each rectangle, color it in, then tell how many squares.

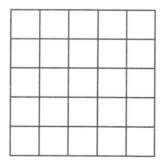

5 × 3 = _____

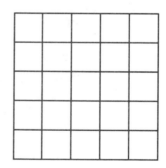

4 × 4 = _____

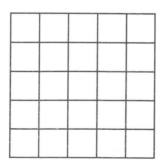

4 × 1 = _____

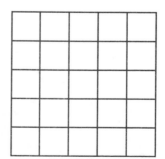

2 × 3 = _____

Helping Children Learn Mathematics, Fifth Edition, © 1998 by Allyn and Bacon

Name: _____

Class: _____

Arranging and Rearranging

▼ Use some counters and string for the rings to make this arrangement:

A   B

• How many counters are in Ring A? _____

• How many counters are in Ring B? _____

▼ Rearrange your counters and rings to show the same numbers, and then move 1 counter from Ring A to Ring B.

• How many counters are now in Ring A? _____

• How many counters are in Ring B? _____

▼ See how many different ways you can put 10 counters in the two rings.

• Use your counters and rings, and list the ways here:

__4+6__   _____   _____   _____

_____   _____   _____   _____

_____   _____   _____

• Plot the ways you listed on graph paper:

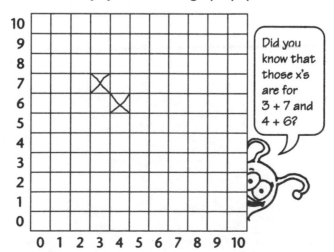

Did you know that those x's are for 3 + 7 and 4 + 6?

Helping Children Learn Mathematics, Fifth Edition, © 1998 by Allyn and Bacon

Name: _____

Class: _____

How Many?

▼ Look at these dots:

- How many groups of dots?
- How many dots in each group?
- How many dots in all?

    Count them: __5__ , ____ , ____ , ____

    Add them: 5 + 5 + 5 + 5 = ☐

    Multiply them: 4 × 5 = ☐

▼ Now look at these dots:

•••••••
•••••••
•••••••
•••••••

- Ring sets of 7. How many sevens?
- How many dots in all?

    Count them: __7__ , ____ , ____ , ____

    Add them: 7 + 7 + 7 + 7 = ☐

    Multiply them: 4 × 7 = ☐

▼ Do these using a calculator:

    7 + 7 + 7 + 7 + 7 = ☐

    5 + 5 + 5 + 5 + 5 = ☐

- Do you know a simpler way? Show it here:

Helping Children Learn Mathematics, Fifth Edition, © 1998 by Allyn and Bacon

Name: _____

Class: _____

Match Up!

▼ Use a set of at least 30 basic subtraction fact cards like these:

▼ Follow these rules:

- The leader deals 5 cards to each player and puts the rest of the cards in the center of the table.

- Players take turns and try to make pairs by matching an example card with an answer card. When a player has a pair, he or she puts them down during a turn.

- Each player may draw 1 card from the center during a turn. When the center cards are gone, the player may draw 1 card from the player to the right.

  When all the cards are used, the player with the most pairs is the winner!

Name: _____

Class: _____

Multig

▼ Use the playing board here or make a larger one on heavy construction paper. Each player needs some buttons, macaroni, or chips for markers.

> Don't forget the spinner. You can't play this game without it!

1. Take turns. Spin twice. Multiply the 2 numbers. Find the answer on the board. Put a marker on it.

56 25 40
36 49 20 81
30 64 35 48 32
56 42 63 28 54 45
32 48 54 72 24 16 35
16 24 28 36 40 30 25 20
63 45 81 56 49 42 64
20 25 72 45 24 36
40 49 32 28 54
30 16 72 48
42 35 63

2. Score 1 point for each covered ◊ that touches a side or corner of the ◊ you cover.

3. If you can't find an uncovered ◊ to cover, you lose your turn.

4. Opponents may challenge any time before the next player spins.

5. The winner is the player with the most points at the end of 10 rounds.

Zero Wins!

▼ Make two identical sets of 19 cards with a number from 0 to 18 on each!

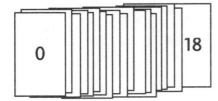 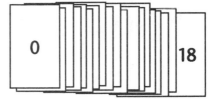

▼ Follow these rules:

• After shuffling, the leader deals 4 cards to each player and puts the remaining cards face down in the center of the table.

• Players must add or subtract the numbers on their 4 cards so they equal 0. For example, suppose you had these cards:

6	10	2	6

$10 - 6 = 4$ or $6 + 6 = 12$
$4 + 2 = 6$ $12 - 12 = 2$
$6 - 6 = 0$ $2 - 2 = 0$

• On each round of play, the players may exchange one card if they wish, and each player takes a turn being first to exchange a card on a round. To make an exchange, the first player draws a card and discards a card, face up. Other players can draw from either the face-down pile or the face-up discard pile.

The first player to get 0 on a round wins the round!

How Would You Do It?

	In your head	With a calculator	With paper/ pencil
60 x 60	☐	☐	☐
945 x 1000	☐	☐	☐
450 x 45	☐	☐	☐
24 x 5 x 2	☐	☐	☐
16,000/2,000	☐	☐	☐
450/45	☐	☐	☐
4 x 15	☐	☐	☐
50 x 17 x 2	☐	☐	☐

Follow Up

▼ Write a computation YOU would solve with a calculator _____

▼ Write a computation YOU would solve mentally _____

▼ Write a computation YOU would solve with paper/pencil _____

Name: _____

Class: _____

How Would You Do It?

	In your head	With a calculator	With paper/pencil
$\frac{1}{2} + \frac{1}{4}$	☐	☐	☐
$1 - \frac{1}{3}$	☐	☐	☐
$\frac{3}{4} + \frac{3}{4}$	☐	☐	☐
$\frac{1}{5} + \frac{1}{6}$	☐	☐	☐
$\frac{1}{2} + \frac{5}{6}$	☐	☐	☐
$1\frac{1}{2} + 2\frac{3}{4}$	☐	☐	☐
$2 - \frac{3}{4}$	☐	☐	☐
$\frac{1}{2} - \frac{1}{3}$	☐	☐	☐

Follow Up

▼ Write a computation YOU would solve with a calculator _____

▼ Write a computation YOU would solve mentally _____

▼ Write a computation YOU would solve with paper/pencil _____

Helping Children Learn Mathematics, Fifth Edition, © 1998 by Allyn and Bacon

Name: _____

Class: _____

Today's Target Is ☐

Try to make today's target in these ways:

1. adding three numbers
2. finding the difference between two numbers
3. multiplying two numbers
4. adding and subtracting
5. using a fraction
6. doing it an unusual way

Name: _____

Class: _____

Compatible Numbers

▼ Find two numbers with a sum of 100.

17	46	15	39
83	61	54	43
92	85	8	75
25	57	80	20

Name: _____

Class: _____

Compatible Numbers

▼ Find two fractions with a sum of 1.

$\frac{1}{4}$	$\frac{2}{3}$	$\frac{7}{8}$	$\frac{5}{8}$
$\frac{1}{2}$	$\frac{1}{10}$	$\frac{3}{4}$	$\frac{5}{10}$
$\frac{3}{8}$	$\frac{1}{8}$	$\frac{5}{12}$	$\frac{9}{10}$
$\frac{7}{12}$	$\frac{3}{10}$	$\frac{1}{3}$	$\frac{7}{10}$

Helping Children Learn Mathematics, Fifth Edition, © 1998 by Allyn and Bacon

Choosing Pairs You Can Work With

Circle the compatible pairs that produce the best estimate.

1. $8\overline{)436}$
↓
$8\overline{)320}$
$8\overline{)400}$
$8\overline{)480}$

2. $7\overline{)8165}$
↓
$7\overline{)700}$
$7\overline{)7000}$
$7\overline{)7700}$

3. $23\overline{)7029}$
↓
$25\overline{)5000}$
$25\overline{)7500}$
$25\overline{)10000}$

4. $42\overline{)8125}$
↓
$40\overline{)10000}$
$40\overline{)8000}$
$40\overline{)80000}$

5. $73\overline{)20162}$
↓
$70\overline{)21000}$
$70\overline{)28000}$
$70\overline{)14000}$

6. $62\overline{)37875}$
↓
$60\overline{)30000}$
$60\overline{)36000}$
$60\overline{)60000}$

Helping Children Learn Mathematics, Fifth Edition, © 1998 by Allyn and Bacon

Name: _____

Class: _____

Starters

▼ Find each missing digit:

$$
\begin{array}{cccc}
52 & 29 & \square 8 & 452 \\
+\ 16 & +\ 36 & +\ 21 & +\ \square 7 \\
\hline
6\square & \square 5 & 79 & 489
\end{array}
$$

▼ Use only the digits given in the cloud to **make a** problem with the sum shown:

$$
\begin{array}{c}
\ \underline{4}\ \ \underline{4} \quad (4,6) \\
+\ \underline{4}\ \ \underline{6} \\
\hline
9\ \ 0
\end{array}
\qquad
\begin{array}{c}
\ \underline{\ }\ \ \underline{\ } \quad (3,5) \\
+\ \underline{\ }\ \ \underline{\ } \\
\hline
8\ \ 8
\end{array}
\qquad
\begin{array}{c}
\ \underline{\ }\ \ \underline{\ } \quad (7,3) \\
+\ \underline{\ }\ \ \underline{\ } \\
\hline
7\ \ 0
\end{array}
$$

▼ Use 2, 4, 6, and 8 for these problems:

• Use each digit once to make the **smallest** sum possible.

• Use each digit once to make **the largest** sum possible.

• Use each digit once to make a sum as **near** 100 as possible.

▼ Use only these numbers:

24	40	22	15	31	14

• Name two numbers whose sum is 64. _____

• Name two numbers whose sum is more than 70. _____

• Name two numbers whose sum ends in 8. _____

• Name three numbers whose sum is 93. _____

Name: _____

Class: _____

Mentally Calculate!

▼ Use only these numbers to answer each question

| 78 | 27 | 39 | 43 | 46 | 15 |

- What two numbers have a difference of

  35?_____ 31?_____ 39?_____

- What two numbers have a difference of

  more than 50?_____ of less than 5?_____

- What number minus 39 gives 7?_____

- What number minus 27 gives 16?_____

- What two numbers have a difference that

  ends in 19?_____ 7?_____

▼ Find the missing weights:

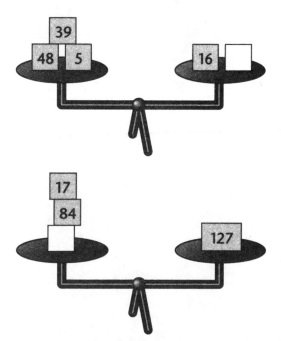

Name: _____

Class: _____

Pattern Search

▼ Write the answer to the last problem in this group:

Can you find a pattern in the answers?

$$\begin{array}{ccccc}
16 & 26 & 46 & 56 & 36 \\
-\ 4 & -\ 4 & -\ 4 & -\ 4 & -\ 4 \\
\hline
12 & 22 & 42 & 52 &
\end{array}$$

▼ Try these:

1.
$$\begin{array}{ccccccc}
18 & 28 & 48 & 38 & 68 & 58 & 98 \\
-\ 2 & -\ 2 & -\ 2 & -\ 2 & -\ 2 & -\ 2 & -\ 2 \\
\hline
\end{array}$$

2.
$$\begin{array}{ccccccc}
18 & 28 & 68 & 38 & 48 & 78 & 58 \\
-\ 9 & -\ 9 & -\ 9 & -\ 9 & -\ 9 & -\ 9 & -\ 9 \\
\hline
\end{array}$$

▼ Complete these subtraction problems:

$$\begin{array}{cccc}
60 & 60 & 60 & 60 \\
-27 & -47 & -17 & -57 \\
\hline
\end{array}$$

• What is alike about each example?

• What is alike about each answer?

• Use the pattern to do these mentally:

$60 - 37 = \boxed{}$ $60 - 7 = \boxed{}$

▼ Now try these:

$43 - 13 = \boxed{}$ $153 - 13 = \boxed{}$

$73 - 13 = \boxed{}$ $123 - 13 = \boxed{}$

$93 - 13 = \boxed{}$ $273 - 13 = \boxed{}$

Name: _____

Class: _____

What's Missing?

▼ Guess the numbers that will go into the circles and boxes.

Write your number and then check it on a . Score 2 points if correct on the first try and 1 point if correct on the second try.

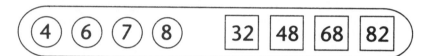

$\bigcirc \times \square = 408$ $\bigcirc \times \square = 384$ $\bigcirc \times \square = 336$

$\bigcirc \times \square = 476$ $\bigcirc \times \square = 272$ $\bigcirc \times \square = 492$

▼ Try these using only 2, 3, and 4:

$$
\begin{array}{c}
\square\,\square \\
\times \quad \square \\
\hline
4 \quad 6
\end{array}
\qquad
\begin{array}{c}
\square\,\square \\
\times \quad \square \\
\hline
6 \quad 6
\end{array}
\qquad
\begin{array}{c}
\square\,\square \\
\times \quad \square \\
\hline
8 \quad 4
\end{array}
\qquad
\begin{array}{c}
\square\,\square \\
\times \quad \square \\
\hline
1 \quad 2 \quad 6
\end{array}
$$

▼ Now use only 4, 6, 8, and 9,

• Make the largest product: $\square\,\square\,\square$
$$\times \qquad \square$$

• Make the smallest product: $\square\,\square\,\square$
$$\times \qquad \square$$

Name: _____

Class: _____

Nines, Nines, Nines . . .

Use your 🖩 to solve these equations.

Write your answers in the blanks.

9 × 1 = _____   9 × 6 = _____   99 × 1 = _____   99 × 6 = _____

9 × 2 = _____   9 × 7 = _____   99 × 2 = _____   99 × 7 = __**693**__

9 × 3 = _____   9 × 8 = _____   99 × 3 = __**297**__   99 × 8 = _____

9 × 4 = _____   9 × 9 = _____   99 × 4 = _____   99 × 9 = _____

9 × 5 = __**45**__   99 × 5 = _____

- What is the sum of the digits in each product? _____

- What is the sum of the first and last digits in each product? _____

- What number is the middle digit in each product? _____

▼ Use your 🖩 to solve these equations. When you see the pattern, try to predict the remaining answers.

   Then use your 🖩 to check.

3 × 9 = __**27**__   5 × 9 = __**45**__   6 × 9 = _____   7 × 9 = _____

3 × 99 = __**297**__   5 × 99 = _____   6 × 99 = _____   7 × 99 = _____

3 × 999 = _____   5 × 999 = _____   6 × 999 = __**5994**__   7 × 999 = _____

3 × 9999 = _____   5 × 9999 = _____   6 × 9999 = _____   7 × 9999 = __**69993**__

3 × 99999 = _____ 5 × 99999 = _____ 6 × 99999 = _____ 7 × 99999 = _____

Helping Children Learn Mathematics, Fifth Edition, © 1998 by Allyn and Bacon

Name: _____

Class: _____

Making Conjectures

▼ Use your calculator:

- Multiply some 2-digit numbers by 99.
  Record your results and make a conjecture.

- Multiply some 3-digit numbers by 999.
  Record your results and make a conjecture.

- Multiply some 2-digit numbers by 999.
  Record your results and make a conjecture.

▼ Now try these.
Find the pattern.

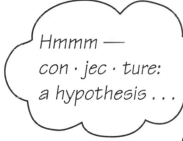

*Hmmm —
con · jec · ture:
a hypothesis . . .*

$$11 \times 11$$
$$111 \times 111$$
$$1111 \times 1111$$

▼ Predict 11111×11111
and check!

Zeros Count

▼ Use your  to find the product:

8 × 10 = _____

- How many 0's in 10? ____
- How many 0's
  in the product? ____

6 × 100 = _____

- How many 0's in 100? ____
- How many 0's in the product? ____

9 × 1000 = _____

- How many 0's in 1000? ____
- How many 0's in the product? ____

▼ Complete this multiplication table. Use your to check your answers.

×	10	100	1000
7			
14		*1400*	
28			*28000*
247			
989			

Name: _____

Class: _____

Number Net

▼ Work with a partner or in a small group to determine the missing values:

Dividend	Divisor	Quotient	Integral Remainder
632	73	____	____
345	____	____	45
____	34	____	27
____	____	____	18
____	746	89	____
7439	____	274	____
____	____	56	73

▼ If the solutions are not unique, explain why not. If no solution is possible, explain why.

- Which combinations result in unique solutions?

- Given any two numbers in a row, can a solution always be found? Why or why not?

- Given only one number in a row, can a solution always be found? Why or why not?

- Which combinations make finding a solution easy? Difficult? Why?

Making Examples

▼ Make a division example with

- A dividend of 47 and a divisor of 3
- A dividend of 81 and a divisor of 5

▼ Now make a division example with

- A quotient of 6 r2
- A quotient of 10 r4
- A quotient of 23 r5

▼ Try these:

- A divisor of 6 and a quotient of 15 r3
- A divisor of 3 and a quotient of 25 r2
- A dividend of 83 and a quotient of 11 r6

How Many Prisms Can You Make?

▼ Use construction paper and masking tape to construct these tubes. Fold and tape each as shown.

- Prism with three congruent faces:

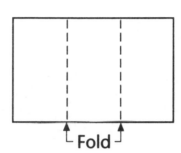 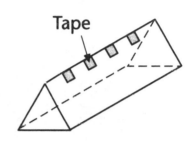

Tape

Fold

- Six-sided prism:

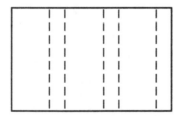 

▼ Your turn:

Try folding and then cutting some others like this one.

Cut   Cut

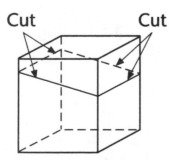 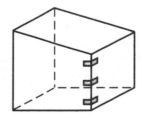

Name: _____

Class: _____

What Can You Discover?

It's easy to complete this table if you've made the tubes on Activity Card 11-3

	Tube 1	Tube 2	Tube 3
Faces	3		
Edges			
Corners			

A. Count the number of faces of Tube 1. (Remember there is no top or bottom, so don't count them.)

B. Count the number of edges of Tube 1. (Don't forget the top and bottom edges.)

C. Repeat A and B for Tube 2.

- Do you see an easy way to tell how many edges if you know the number of faces?_____

- Write your conjecture: _____

_____

D. Count the corners of Tube 1 and Tube 2.

- Do you see an easy way to tell how many corners if you know the number of faces and edges?_____

- Write your conjecture: _____

_____

Check your conjecture with Tube 3.

Helping Children Learn Mathematics, Fifth Edition, © 1998 by Allyn and Bacon

Name: _____

Class: _____

Build Your Own Pyramid!

▼ Follow these easy steps to construct a "stick" pyramid from newspaper. Use masking tape for the connectors.

Step 1: Take three sheets from a newspaper and roll tightly from corner to corner.

Roll

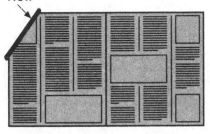

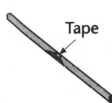

Tape

Step 2: Tape to hold rod.

Step 3: Make several rods and tape together as shown.

Tape

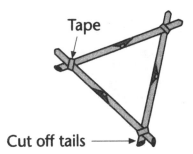

Cut off tails ⟶

Step 4: Put them together to make a pyramid.

▼ Your turn:

Use the same method to construct other three-dimensional shapes, such as a cube.

Name: _____

Class: _____

Less Is Best
(A game for two or more)

▼ Choose a partner to play this game:

 • Put an assortment of pattern blocks in a box.

 • Without looking, each player chooses 3 blocks and puts them together to make a new shape.

 • Count the number of sides on each of the new shapes. Whoever has the shape with the fewest sides wins—less is best!

▼ Make a table to record your scores, and play several rounds to determine the winner.

Me	4			
You	4			

Name: _____

Class: _____

Show My Sides

▼ Use a geoboard to show these figures:

1. Can you make a 4-sided figure with exactly two equal sides?

2. Can you make a 12-sided figure with all sides equal?

3. Can you make a 3-sided figure with three equal sides?

4. Can you make an 8-sided figure with four sides of one length and the other four of another length?

5. Can you make a 5-sided figure with exactly four equal sides?

6. Can you make a 4-sided figure with two pairs of equal sides that is not a parallelogram?

7. Can you make a 3-sided figure with two equal sides?

8. Can you make a 7-sided figure with no equal sides?

Name: _____

Class: _____

Exploring with Logo

▼ Use a Logo program. You will need to know the following commands before trying this activity. If you do not, explore these first.

```
FORWARD (FD), RIGHT (RT), HOME,
SHOW TURTLE (ST), CLEARSCREEN (CS)
```

▼ Identify each of these figures. Write your guess and then draw the figure. Don't forget to CS after each figure is identified.

A _____	B _____	C _____	D _____
HOME	HOME	HOME	HOME
FD 40	FD 40	FD 40	RT 120
RT 90	RT 60	RT 120	FD 40
FD 20	FD 40	FD 40	RT 120
RT 90	RT 60	RT 120	FD 40
FD 40	FD 40	RT 40	RT 120
RT 90			FD 40
FD 20			

▼ Try the following:

1. REPEAT 4 [FD 40 RT 90]

• What did you draw? _____

2. [RT 45 REPEAT 4 [FD 40 RT 90]

• What is the difference between 1 and 2? _____

3. REPEAT 3 [FD 40 RT 120]

• Have you drawn this one before? _____

▼ See if you can draw a hexagon.

• What did you tell the turtle to do? _____

▼ For fun try these:

```
TO BOX                          TO BOXES
REPEAT 4 [FD 40 RT 90]          REPEAT 8 [BOX RT 45]
END                             END
BOX                             BOXES
CS
```

Name: _____

Class: _____

Piezles

▼ Solve these *piezles* (puzzles) using pattern blocks.
Draw a sketch of the shape you made.

1. Use two different pieces; make a shape with

- Exactly 2 pairs of parallel sides.

- Exactly 1 pair of parallel sides.

- No parallel sides.

2. Use three different pieces; make a shape with

- Exactly 3 pairs of parallel sides.

- Exactly 2 pair of parallel sides.

- Exactly 1 pair of parallel sides.

- No parallel sides.

3. What is the largest number of pairs of parallel sides of a shape you can make from

- 2 pieces?

- 3 pieces?

- 4 pieces?

4. Can you put all the pieces together to make a shape with no parallel sides?

Helping Children Learn Mathematics, Fifth Edition, © 1998 by Allyn and Bacon

Name: _____

Class: _____

What's My Altitude?

▼ Make a triangle from a stiff piece of paper. Cut a strip 2 cm by 20 cm. Mark off segments of 9 cm, 4 cm, and 7 cm and label them A, B, and C, respectively. Fold and tape as shown:

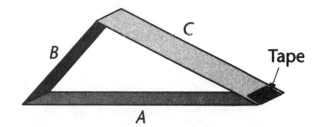

1. Set the triangle on side A. This is the base.

   • How long is the base? ____9 cm____

   • What is the altitude? _____

   • How long is the altitude? _____

2. Set the triangle on side B. This is the base now.

   • How long is the base? _____

   • What is the altitude? _____

   • How long is the altitude? _____

3. Set the triangle on side C. This is the base now.

   • How long is the base? _____

   • What is the altitude? _____

   • How long is the altitude? _____

▼ On a large sheet of paper: Trace the triangle and show the altitude for each of the bases.

Name: _____

Class: _____

The Triangle Experiment

▼ Follow these directions:

Step 1: Draw a triangle.
Cut it out.

Step 2: Find, by folding, the
midpoint of each side.

Step 3: Join the midpoints.

Step 4: Cut apart the 4 triangles.

• What did you find? _____

▼ Try another triangle.

• Did the same thing happen? _____

▼ Try an isosceles triangle.

• What are the small triangles? _____

▼ Try an equilateral triangle.

• What are the small triangles? _____

• What is your conjecture? _____

Name: _____

Class: _____

Classify Me

▼ Mark each of the figures with a

1. if it is a quadrilateral,

2. if it has two pairs of parallel sides,

3. if it has all right angles,

4. if it has all congruent sides.

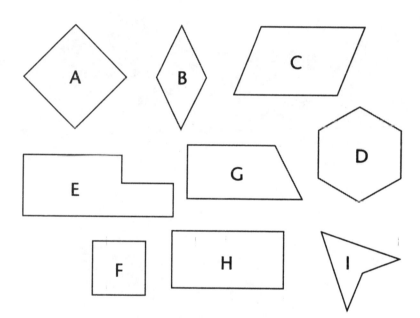

• Any figure marked 1 and 2 is a _____

• Any figure marked 1, 2, and 3
  is a rectangle as well as a _____

• Any figure marked 1, 2, and 4 is a _____

  as well as a _____

• Any figure marked 1, 2, 3, and 4 is a _____

  and a _____ as well as a square.

Name: _____

Class: _____

Can You Find It?

▼ See if you can find each of these in the design. Fill in the shape, and mark it with the matching letter.

    A. triangle—isosceles

    B. triangle—scalene

    C. quadrilateral—not symmetric

    D. quadrilateral—4 lines of symmetry

    E. pentagon—concave

    F. pentagon—convex

    G. hexagon—exactly 2 pairs of parallel sides

    H. hexagon—symmetric

    I. heptagon (7 sides)—symmetric

    J. heptagon—not symmetric

    K. octagon

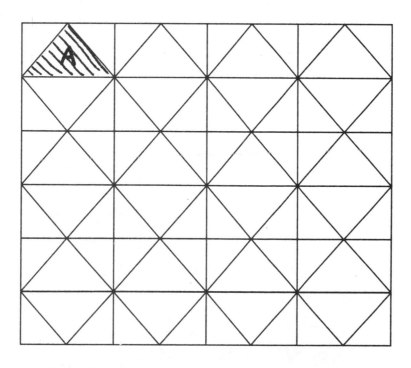

Activity Card 12–1

Name: _____

Class: _____

Problem? Solve It!

Length   Grade 2

▼ Cut a strip of paper:

30 cm

| 2 cm

▼ Measure 5 cm from one end and fold:

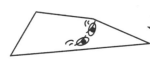

fold

▼ Put away the ruler.

▼ Fold the whole strip to make a rectangle with the 5 cm as one side.

5 cm

Area   Grade 4

▼ Take 4 squares of the same size.

How many rectangles can you make?

▼ Make as many other figures with area of 4 squares as you can by putting the squares side by side like

this   not this

Angles   Grade 6

I'm a closed figure with 2 acute angles and 2 obtuse.

Can you draw a closed figure with

• 2 right angles, 1 acute angle, and 1 obtuse angle?

• 3 right angles and 2 other angles?

• 2 right angles and 2 acute angles?

• 1 right angle, 1 acute angle, and 1 obtuse angle?

Volume   Grade 8

8 cm

4 cm

3 cm

You can change one dimension of this rectangular solid by 1 cm.

• Which dimension would you change to change the volume

the most?_____ the least?_____

Try another rectangular solid.

• What is your hypothesis?

Helping Children Learn Mathematics, Fifth Edition, © 1998 by Allyn and Bacon

Name: _____

Class: _____

Areas, Areas, Areas

▼ Study how one person found the area of an odd shape:

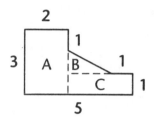

A: 6
B: 1
C: 3
‾‾‾‾
10 square units

▼ Use a method to find the area of each of these shapes:

A

B

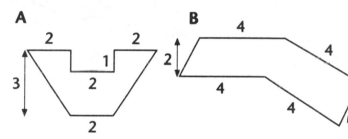

C

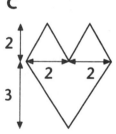

D

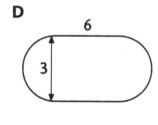

E   **F**

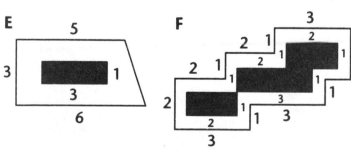

▼ Your turn:

Design your own strange shape and show how to find its area.

Name: _____

Class: _____

What's My Area?

▼ Each triangle is half of a parallelogram.

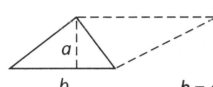 or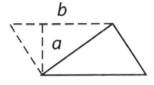

b = 4, a = 2

Area of parallelogram = 8 square units, so
Area of triangle = 4 square units.

▼ Use this method to find the area for each triangle.
(You can trace the triangle, cut out the copy, and
move it to make the parallelogram.)

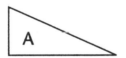

Area = _____

Area = _____

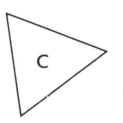

Area = _____

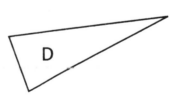

Area = _____

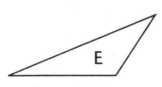

Area = _____

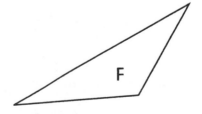

Area = _____

Helping Children Learn Mathematics, Fifth Edition, © 1998 by Allyn and Bacon

Name: _____

Class: _____

What's My Area
When I Change My Shape?

▼ Using graph paper, color and label some squares:

I'm only one shape.

Together we make a lot of shapes.

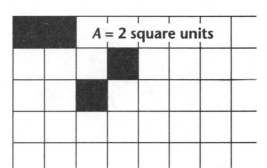

A = 2 square units

▼ See how many different shapes you can make that are the same area.

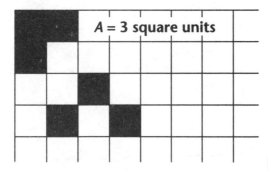

A = 3 square units

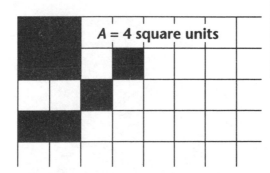

A = 4 square units

Don't forget to use the same number of squares for each new shape.

Name: _____

Class: _____

Same Volume, Different Shape

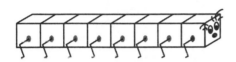 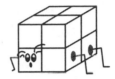

I'm 8 cubes — 8 by 1 by 1.
My volume is
8 square units.

I'm 8 cubes — 2 by 2 by 2.
My volume is
8 square units, too!

▼ See how many different rectangular solids you can make with 12 cubes. Record the dimensions and volume of each.

▼ Now try some of these:

7, 9, 16, 11, 13, 18, 15 cubes

▼ How many different solids can you make if the number of cubes is

• prime? _____

• a product of two primes? _____

• a perfect square? _____

▼ How many solids can you make with

24 cubes? _____

Name: _____

Class: _____

Do You Know How to Connect Perimeter and Area?

▼ Cut a string 14 cm long, and use stick pins to attach it to graph paper.

▼ How many different rectangles can you make with a perimeter of 14 cm? Find the area of each.

I see you followed the rules and made each side a whole number.

Here's one that I made.

Now try 20 cm. What about 13 cm? What about 17 cm? What about . . .

$P = 14$ cm
$A = 10$ cm^2

Name: _____

Class: _____

What Is the Connection between Volume and Area?

▼ Use construction paper to make two tubes:

A.

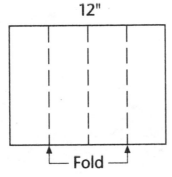

12"

9"

Fold

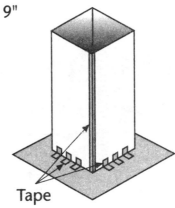

Tape

B.

12"

9"

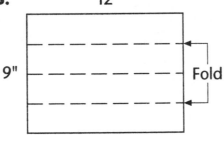

Fold

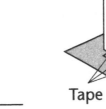

Tape

▼ Guess which tube holds more, or do they hold the same? _____

▼ Fill and see.

Name: _____

Class: _____

What Is the Connection between Perimeter and Height?

▼ Cut 6 strips (2 cm by 21 cm) from stiff paper.

▼ Fold one strip into thirds, and tape together to make a fence triangle:

Tape

▼ Fold the other strips into fourths, fifths, sixths, sevenths, and eighths to make additional fences.

▼ Fill it in the chart:

Number of sides	Length of each side in mm	Height (stand it on one side and see how tall)
3	_____ mm	_____ mm
4	_____	_____
5	_____	_____
6	_____	_____
7	_____	_____
8	_____	_____

• Which has the largest area?

• Which has the smallest area?

Name: _____

Class: _____

Metric to Metric

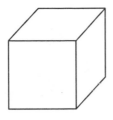   

1 dm^3 1 liter (l)

Capacity and Volume

▼ Fill the liter measure with water, and pour it into the cubic decimeter.

What did you find?

1 liter = _____ cubic decimeters

Remember: 1 liter = 1000 milliliters (ml)

1 cubic decimeter (dm^3) =
1000 cubic meter (cm^3)

Therefore, 1 ml has a volume of _____ cm^3

Weight and Capacity

▼ Weigh the liter of water.

What did you find?

1 liter = _____ kg of water

Remember: 1 liter = 1000 milliliters (ml)

1 kilogram = 1000 grams (g)

Therefore, 1 ml has a volume of _____ g of water

Weight and Volume

▼ Use your findings:

1 cubic decimeter = _____ kg of water

1 cubic centimeter = _____ g of water

Helping Children Learn Mathematics, Fifth Edition, © 1998 by Allyn and Bacon

Name: _____

Class: _____

Whole Hog

▼ Choose a partner, and each of you make your own gameboard by tracing the H (for Hog):

▼ Cut ten squares of paper. Write one of these fractions on each square:

$$\frac{1}{2} \quad \frac{1}{3} \quad \frac{1}{6} \quad \frac{2}{6} \quad \frac{1}{9} \quad \frac{2}{9} \quad \frac{3}{9} \quad \frac{1}{18} \quad \frac{2}{18} \quad \frac{3}{18}$$

▼ Be sure each of you has a crayon.

Now you are ready to go Whole Hog!

Game Rules

1. Put the fraction cards in a pile face down.

2. Each of you pick a card from the top of the pile.

3. Turn your cards over and decide who has the larger fraction.

4. The player with the larger fraction must color that fractional part of her or his H.

5. Put both cards at the bottom of the pile.

6. Choose two or more cards and play as before.

7. If a player with the larger fraction cannot color the fractional part shown on the card, both players must put their cards back and pick two more.

8. Continue playing until one person colors the whole H. That person is the first to go Whole Hog and loses the game.

Name: _____

Class: _____

Think, Think, Think!

To find equivalent mixed numbers and fractions without using pictures, you can think of whole numbers that are equivalent to fractions:

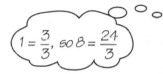

$1 = \dfrac{3}{3}$, so $8 = \dfrac{24}{3}$

$\dfrac{8}{8} = 1$, so $\dfrac{24}{8} = 3$

$8\dfrac{2}{3} = \dfrac{24}{3} + \dfrac{2}{3} = \dfrac{26}{3}$

$\dfrac{27}{8} = \dfrac{24}{8} + \dfrac{3}{8} = 3\dfrac{3}{8}$

▼ Try these. (Remember, no pictures allowed.)

1.
$1 = \dfrac{\square}{4}$, so $5 = \dfrac{\square}{4}$

$5\dfrac{3}{4} = \dfrac{\square}{4}$

2.
$\dfrac{\square}{5} = 1$, so $\dfrac{40}{5} = \square$

$\dfrac{43}{5} = \square\dfrac{\square}{5}$

3.
$1 = \dfrac{\square}{6}$, so $7 = \dfrac{\square}{6}$

$7\dfrac{5}{6} = \dfrac{\square}{6}$

4.
$\dfrac{\square}{9} = 1$, so $\dfrac{18}{9} = \square$

$\dfrac{20}{9} = \square\dfrac{\square}{9}$

5.
$1 = \dfrac{\square}{3}$, so $4 = \dfrac{\square}{3}$

$4\dfrac{1}{3} = \dfrac{\square}{3}$

6.
$\dfrac{\square}{7} = 1$, so $\dfrac{21}{7} = \square$

$\dfrac{22}{7} = \square\dfrac{\square}{7}$

7.
$1 = \dfrac{\square}{10}$, so $7 = \dfrac{\square}{10}$

$7\dfrac{6}{10} = \dfrac{\square}{10}$

8.
$\dfrac{\square}{5} = 1$, so $\dfrac{15}{5} = \square$

$\dfrac{18}{5} = \square\dfrac{\square}{5}$

Activity Card 13–5

Name: _____

Class: _____

Painting Problems

▼ Several artists were painting unusual pictures. Use their pictures to help you answer the questions.

Untitled #1

This painter painted $\frac{1}{4}$ of his painting. He rested and then painted $\frac{3}{8}$ more. How much did he paint altogether?

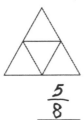

$$\frac{5}{8}$$

Untitled #2

This painter carefully painted $\frac{2}{4}$ of the painting. Then she painted $\frac{1}{2}$ more of it. How much did she paint altogether? _____

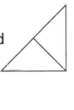

Untitled #3

After this painter had done $\frac{2}{3}$ of this painting, he found he had made a mistake and had to scrape off $\frac{2}{6}$. How much was still painted? _____

Untitled #4

This painter painted $\frac{3}{4}$ of her canvas yellow. She then scraped the paint off $\frac{1}{2}$ of her canvas. How much was still painted? _____

Untitled #5

First, $\frac{3}{8}$ of this lovely canvas was painted. Then $\frac{3}{8}$ more was painted. How much was painted altogether? _____

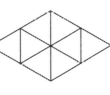

Untitled #6

After this artist finished $\frac{1}{3}$ of the painting, he decided that he didn't like it, so he scraped the paint off $\frac{2}{9}$ of it. How much was left painted? _____

Untitled #7

This painter painted $\frac{3}{10}$ of her canvas upside down and $\frac{2}{5}$ of it right side up. How much did she paint altogether? _____

Untitled #8

This painting was damaged by a low-flying bird when $\frac{2}{3}$ of it was done. So $\frac{4}{6}$ had to be repainted. How much of the painted part was not damaged? _____

Helping Children Learn Mathematics, Fifth Edition, © 1998 by Allyn and Bacon

Name: _____

Class: _____

Plug-In Puzzles

▼ Use these decimal fractions to fill in the blanks.

   8.3   4.2   5.5   3.1   7.6   6.7

Do each multiplication or
division. In the division
problems, divide to
the hundredths
place. Sum the
four answers.

___ × ___ = _____

___ ÷ 5 = _____

___ × ___ = _____

___ ÷ 3 = _____

Total _____

- What is the largest total you can get? _____

- Can you get a total greater than 50? _____

- Can you get one greater than 100? _____

▼ Arrange these four decimals in the boxes so that
the sentence is true. (Remember to do the parts in
the parentheses first.)

   5.13   4.24   3.84   3.16

$$\left(\underline{\quad} \times 5 \right) + \underline{\quad} = \left(4 \times \underline{\quad} \right) + \underline{\quad}$$

▼ Pick the two decimals from those listed that will
make the sentence true.

   21.21   42.42   36.36   63.63   27.27

$$\left(\underline{\quad} \div 7 \right) \times 8 = \left(\underline{\quad} \div 9 \right) \times 6$$

Name: _____

Class: _____

Know Your Coins

▼ Use patterns to help complete this table:

Number of

Quarters	1	2		4	5	6	□
Nickels	5	10	15	20		30	△
Pennies	25	50	75		125	150	○

- Describe a pattern you found in each row.

- Write a ratio for the number of quarters to nickels. _____

- Write a ratio for the number of nickels to pennies. _____

- Write a ratio for the number of quarters to pennies. _____

▼ Try these:

- How many nickels will be needed for 8 quarters? _____
  Tell two different ways to decide.

- How many pennies will be needed for 10 quarters? _____
  Tell two different ways to decide.

- Give three numbers (not shown in the table) that could go

  in the △ row _____   in the ○ row _____

- Give three numbers that could *not* go

  in the △ row _____   in the ○ row _____

- How many quarters would you have

  when □ + △ + ○ first exceeds $50? _____

Helping Children Learn Mathematics, Fifth Edition, © 1998 by Allyn and Bacon

Name: _____

Class: _____

How Do You Solve Proportion Problems?

Method 1

3 : 12 = 5 : ☐
bags things   bags things

There are 3 bags and 12 things. The second number is 4 times the first. 3 x 4 = 12 so 5 x 4 = 20

x4 ⌒ x4 ⌒
3:12 = 5: 20
bags things bags things

Method 2

6 : 26 = 3 : ☐
bags things   bags things

How many things in a bag? The second number is how many times the first? That's not easy to figure out.

Hmmm, 26 things in 6 bags. 3 bags is ½ of 6 bags. So there have to be ½ of 26 things.
6 ÷ 2 = 3   26 ÷ 2 = 13

6 ÷ 2 ⌒ 26 ÷ 2
6:26 = 3: 13
bags things bags things

Solve the following proportions. Use whatever method is easiest for you.

A. 20 : 30 = 40 : ☐
doors walls   doors walls

B. 9 : 81 = 15 : ☐
teams players   teams players

C. 15 : 30 = 220 : ☐
books pupils   books pupils

D. 43 : 13 = ☐ : 39
horses owners   horses owners

E. 24 : 8 = 27 : ☐
fish gulls   fish gulls

F. 5 : 16 = ☐ : 32
dogs tricks   dogs tricks

G. 8 : 56 = ☐ : 21
workers $ workers $

H. 11 : ☐ = 8 : 64
kg objects   kg objects

I. 48 : 14 = 24 : ☐
ml tubes   ml tubes

J. 500 : 25 = 100 : ☐
liters cans   liters cans

K. ☐ : 8 = 12 : 32
bars ¢   bars ¢

L. 100 : ☐ = 12 : 3
tacks ¢   tacks ¢

Name: _____

Class: _____

Using Percents

A. Color this circle:

- 25% red

- 50% blue

What percent is uncolored? _____

B. Use 3 colors:

- Blue

- Green

- Yellow

Color each
log with only
one color.
Color all logs.

	Number Colored	Percent Colored
Blue	_____	_____
Green	_____	_____
Yellow	_____	_____

C. Take 100 pennies,
shake, and toss them
in a box. Count the
number of heads.

	Number	Percent
Heads	_____	_____
Tails	_____	_____

Did you need
to count the tails? _____

D. Here are 20 poker chips. Count the number of
each color.

	Number	Percent
Blue	_____	_____
Black	_____	_____
White	_____	_____

Helping Children Learn Mathematics, Fifth Edition, © 1998 by Allyn and Bacon

Name: _____

Class: _____

What Are the Chances?

▼ Sort these statements into the best box.

Impossible	Unlikely	Likely	Certain

A. The sun will rise in the west.

B. The cafeteria will serve chocolate milk.

C. A boy in our class will be 2 meters tall.

D. Everyone in this room is alive.

E. Most people in our class have brown eyes.

F. There are more right-handed people in this room than left-handed.

G. The price of gas will be higher next year.

H. It will rain today.

Explain your reasons for each.

Name: _____

Class: _____

Random Winner!

Our class is having a drawing. Each person gets to place their name in the drawing one time. One name will be randomly picked, and that person will be the winner.

- ▾ Read each of the following statements.
- ▾ Think about the people in our class.
- ▾ Then, check the number line below and decide about where the following statements should be placed:

A. The winner will be left handed.

B. The winner will be a girl.

C. The winner will be someone in our class.

D. The number of letters in the first name of the winner will be less than the number of letters in their last name.

E. The winner's first name will begin with a vowel.

F. The winner will wear glasses.

G. You will be the winner.

H. The winner will be wearing socks.

I. You will not be the winner.

```
├───────────────┼───────────────┼───────────────┤
0                                .5 or ½                         1
Impossible                                         Certain to happen
```

Helping Children Learn Mathematics, Fifth Edition, © 1998 by Allyn and Bacon

Name: _____

Class: _____

Can You Make Predictions?

▼ Roll a die six times and record the results:

1	2	3	4	5	6

• Did each face appear once? _____

• Does knowing what happened on the first roll

   help predict the second? _____

   the third? _____

▼ Roll a die 24 times and record the results.

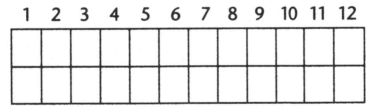

1	2	3	4	5	6	7	8	9	10	11	12

13 14 15 16 17 18 19 20 21 22 23 24

• Did each face appear once?_____

   the same number of times?_____

• What face appeared most?_____

   Does this mean the die is unfair?_____

   Does this record tell you
   what will occur on the next roll?_____

Name: _____

Class: _____

Check Your Probability Knowledge

> This bag has three red balls, one white ball, and one black ball.

Sample space:

- How many balls are in the bag?

- What color balls could be drawn?

- Must a ball be returned to the bag after it has been drawn? (This, of course, depends on the questions being asked.)

Probability of an event:

- What is the probability of drawing a red ball?

- What is the probability of drawing a ball that is not red?

- What is the probability of drawing a black or white ball?

- What is the probability of drawing a green ball?

- What is the probability of drawing a red, black, or white ball?

Randomness:

- Should the red balls be placed at the bottom of the bag and the black and white balls placed on top of them?

- Should the bag be shaken before each draw?

- Should people be allowed to choose their favorite color?

- Should people be allowed to pick several balls and then choose their favorite?

- Should the person choosing be blindfolded?

- Should a transparent bag be used?

Independence:

- If a white ball has just been drawn and returned to the bag, what is the probability the next ball will be white?

- If four consecutive red balls have been drawn and returned each time to the bag, what is the probability the next ball will be red?

Create a Design!

▼ Color one to three triangles of the top left square in each Design A–D

Design A

Design B

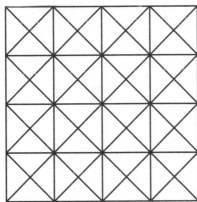

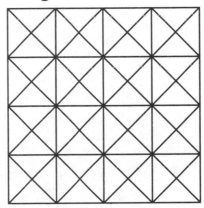

Design C

Design D

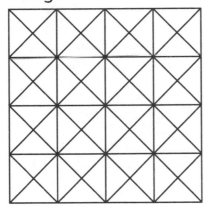

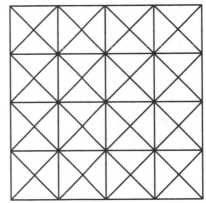

- For Design A, color each square the same way you did the first square.

- For Design B, color each square in the first row the same way. Color the next row the opposite way. Repeat.

- For Design C, color the first square in the first row. Color the second square the opposite way. Repeat for rows and columns.

- For Design D, make up your own pattern.

Activity Card 16–2

Name: _____

Class: _____

Square Designs

▼ Look at these designs made by sixth-grade students. The students began with the segmented square shown, colored part of it, and then flipped, turned, or slid it to the next square.

  • For each pattern, tell which motion was used and the number of squares in the core (that is, the number of squares before the pattern repeats).

A. Motion: _____

  Number of squares in core: _____

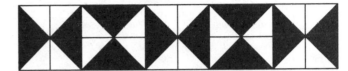

B. Motion: _____

  Number of squares in core: _____

C. Motion: _____

  Number of squares in core: _____

D. Motion: _____

  Number of squares in core: _____

E. Motion: _____

  Number of squares in core: _____

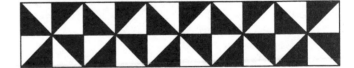

F. Motion: _____

  Number of squares in core: _____

▼ Your turn:

  • Begin with this square:
  • Color part of it.
  • Flip, turn, or slide.

Helping Children Learn Mathematics, **Fifth Edition**, © 1998 by Allyn and Bacon

Name: _____

Class: _____

What Do You See in Me?

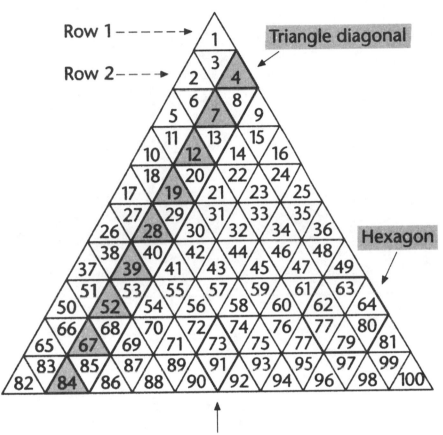

Row 1 - - - - - →

Row 2 - - - →

Triangle diagonal

Hexagon

Diamond column

- Do you see the perfect squares?

- Where are the odd numbers?

- Find the sum of the numbers in each row. See if you can find a shortcut. [*Hint:* Factor the sums of several rows.]

- Take any hexagon. What is its sum? Can you find a shortcut?

- Take any two adjacent numbers in a triangle diagonal (for example, 4 and 7). Find their product. Where is it?

Do You Believe That?

▼ Try one of these conjectures about positive whole numbers. See if you can find examples that disprove each.

- *Tinbach's Conjecture:* Every number can be expressed as the difference of two primes.

  Examples: $14 = 17 - 3$ $5 = 7 - 2$ $28 = 31 - 3$

- *Zinbach's Conjecture:* Every number can be expressed as the sum of 3 squares (0 is permitted).

  Examples: $3 = 1^2 + 1^2 + 1^2$ $14 = 1^2 + 2^2 + 3^2$
  $9 = 3^2 + 0^2 + 0^2$

- *Aluminumbach's Conjecture:* Every odd number can be expressed as the sum of 3 primes.

  Examples: $15 = 5 + 5 + 5$ $11 = 3 + 3 + 5$

- *Brassbach's Conjecture:* Every square number has exactly 3 divisors.

  Example: $2^2 = 4$, 4 has 3 divisors 1, 2, and 4

- *Copperbach's Conjecture:* The product of any number of primes is odd.

  Examples: $5 \times 3 \times 7 = 105$ (3 primes)
  $7 \times 3 \times 3 \times 5 = 315$ (4 primes)

Am I Abundant, Deficient, or Perfect?

▼ How to tell:

- Find all the divisors of the number, except itself, and add those divisors.

- If the sum is *greater* than the number, then the number is **abundant**.

- If the sum is *less* than the number, then the number is **deficient**.

- If the sum is *equal* to the number, then the number is **perfect**.

▼ Examples:

35   1 + 5 + 7 = 13   13 < 35   deficient

18   1 + 2 + 3 + 6 + 9 = 21   21 > 18   abundant

28   1 + 2 + 4 + 7 + 14 = 28   28 = 28   perfect

▼ Your turn:

Classify the numbers 1–20.

Find 5 abundant numbers.

▼ Challenge:

What is 496?

▼ Superchallenge:

What is 8128?

Factor Me Out

▼ Choose a partner and make a chart to play this game:

●	2	3	4	5	6
7	8	9	10	11	12
13	14	15	16	17	18
19	20	21	22	23	24
25	26	27	28	29	30
31	32	33	34	35	36

▼ Rules:

- Player 1 chooses a number. He or she gets that many points. The opponent gets points equal to the sum of all the factors.

- Make a table to record scores:

Player 1	Player 2
10	7 (2 + 5)

- Mark out the number and the factors; these cannot be used again.

- Repeat with Player 2 choosing the number.

- Alternate turns until no numbers are left.

The player with the most points wins.

Helping Children Learn Mathematics, Fifth Edition, © 1998 by Allyn and Bacon

Name: _____

Class: _____

Pascal's Triangle

▼ Finish row 7 of this triangle.

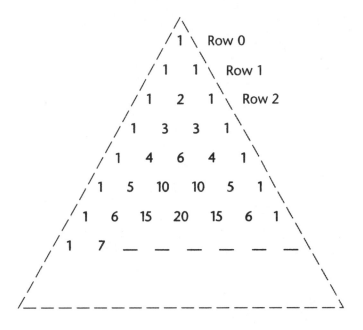

▼ Write rows 8 and 9.

• What patterns do you see?

▼ Find the sum of each row, by filling in the table:

Row	Sum
0	1
1	1 + 1 = 2
2	1 + 2 + 1 = 4
3	
4	
5	

▼ Guess before you calculate:

• What do you think the sum of the eighth row is?

• How about the twentieth row?

▼ Look at the numbers in any odd row (ignore the ones):

• What do you notice?

• Do you think this will be true in row 9?

Activity Card 16–10

Name: _____

Class: _____

Generate It!

This program generates Fibonacci numbers!

▼ Run the following program:

```
 1 REM FIBONACCI NUMBERS
10 DIM F(30)
20 F(1) = 1: F(2) = 1
30 FOR N = 3 TO 30: F(N) =
   F (N-1) + F(N-2)
40 PRINT "F(N)="; F(N)
50 NEXT N
60 END
```

▼ Modify the program as follows:

• To generate the Lucas sequence:
  1, 3, 4, 7, 11, . . .

• To generate the first 50 Fibonacci numbers.

• To generate the first sequence 1, 2, 3, 6, 11, 20, . . . [*Hint:* 11 = 2 + 3 + 6.]

• To generate the sequence 1, 2, 3, 4, 10, 19, 36, . . .

Look for patterns:

• What Fibonacci number divides F(5), F(10), F(15)? _____

• What Fibonacci number divides F(3), F(6), F(9)? _____

• What Fibonacci number divides F(6), F(12), F(18)? _____

• If L(N) is the *n*th Lucas Number, what does L(N)*F(N+1) − F(N)*L(N+1) equal? _____

Name: _____

Class: _____

Count Those Rectangles!

▼ How many rectangles in this figure?

```
┌──┬──┬──┬──┬──┬──┬──┬──┬──┬──┬──┬──┬──┬──┬──┐
├──┼──┼──┼──┼──┼──┼──┼──┼──┼──┼──┼──┼──┼──┼──┤
└──┴──┴──┴──┴──┴──┴──┴──┴──┴──┴──┴──┴──┴──┴──┘
```

▼ If you want some hints, try this.

▼ Begin with a smaller problem:

       1 square
       <u>0</u> nonsquare rectangles
       1 total

       2 squares
       <u>1</u> nonsquare rectangles
       3 total

       3 squares
       <u>3</u> nonsquare rectangles
       6 total

▼ Continue with 4 squares, 5 squares, and on.

▼ Complete the table:

- Fill in Row A of the table with the number of squares.

- Fill in Row B with the number of rectangles that are not squares.

- Find the total for each column and fill in Row C.

Look for a pattern to help you!

A	1	2	3	4	5	6								
B	0	1	3											
C	1	3	6											

Helping Children Learn Mathematics, Fifth Edition, © 1998 by Allyn and Bacon

Name: _____

Class: _____

Sieve 6

▼ Do it:

- Circle 2, then mark out every second number.

- Circle 3, then mark out every third number (6, 9, 12, . . .) Some may already be marked out.

- Circle 5 (since 4 is marked out) and mark out every fifth number. Continue to 96.

②	3	✗	5	✗	
7	✗	9	10	11	12
13	14	15	16	17	18
19	20	21	22	23	24
25	26	27	28	29	30
31	32	33	34	35	36
37	38	39	40	41	42
43	44	45	46	47	48
49	50	51	52	53	54
55	56	57	58	59	60
61	62	63	64	65	66
67	68	69	70	71	72
73	74	75	76	77	78
79	80	81	82	83	84
85	86	87	88	89	90
91	92	93	94	95	96

▼ Talk about it:

- What numbers are circled? _____

- In what columns are they? _____